More Praise for *Francis of Assisi: Writer and Spiritual Master* by Thaddée Matura

"From a lifetime dedicated to the spiritual way of Saint Francis, Brother Thaddée has distilled an admirable summary of the profound spirituality of a simple, uneducated man…. The author clearly speaks as a practitioner of the tradition he describes, adding a personal warmth and depth to his descriptions of Francis. A beautifully crafted and heartfelt treatment of Francis' spirituality."

> Brother William Short, O.F.M.
> Professor of Christian Spirituality
> Franciscan School of Theology, Berkeley, California

"Every member of the Franciscan family and everyone whose hearts warm to the figure of Francis of Assisi will find here a real treasure… Thaddée's synthesis of Francis' teaching leads us back to the 'spring of living water welling up to eternal life' and opens for us the purity of what may, in the fullest sense, be called the Eternal Gospel."

> Seán Collins, O.F.M.
> Irish Franciscan Province
> Former Member, General Council of the Order

FRANCIS ᴏꜰ ASSISI

WRITER
and
SPIRITUAL
MASTER

Thaddée Matura, O.F.M.

Translated by Paul Lachance, O.F.M.
with the collaboration of Colette Wisnewski

ST. ANTHONY MESSENGER PRESS

Cincinnati, Ohio

This is a translation of *François d'Assise, maître de vie spirituelle* by Thaddée Matura, O.F.M., published by Les Editions Franciscaines, Paris, copyright ©2000.

We are grateful for permission to quote material printed by the following publishers:

Scripture citations, unless otherwise indicated as translations of Saint Francis, are taken from the *New Revised Standard Version Bible*, copyright ©1989 by the Division of Christian Education of the National Council of Churches in the United States of America and used by permission. All Rights Reserved.

Excerpts from *Francis of Assisi: Early Documents, Volume 1*, edited by Regis J. Armstrong, J. A. Wayne Hellmann and William J. Short, copyright ©1999. Reprinted with the permission of New City Press.

Cover design by Mark Sullivan
Cover painting: *Saint Francis Praying* by Francisco de Zurbaran (1598-1664)
Licensed from SuperStock
Interior design by Phillips Robinette, O.F.M.

Library of Congress Cataloging-in-Publication Data

Matura, Thaddée.
    [François d'Assise. English]
    Francis of Assisi : writer and spiritual master / Thaddée Matura ; translated by Paul Lachance ; with the collaboration of Colette Wisnewski.
        p. cm.
 Includes bibliographical references.
 ISBN 0-86716-660-6 (alk. paper)
1. Francis, of Assisi, Saint, 1182-1226. 2. Spirituality—History—Middle Ages, 600-1500. I. Wisnewski, Colette. II. Title.
    BX4700.F6M356613 2005
    271'.302—dc22

                              2004025764

ISBN 0-86716-660-6

Published by St. Anthony Messenger Press
28 W. Liberty St., Cincinnati, OH 45202
www.AmericanCatholic.org
Printed in the United States of America

05 06 07 08 09 10 5 4 3 2 1

To my Franciscan brothers who make my work,
including this translation, possible.

TABLE OF CONTENTS

FOREWORD

Many people probably know of Francis of Assisi most commonly as the saint who could talk to the birds (and, of course, they were listening) and who tamed a ferocious wolf. Since medieval times an abundance of literature has generated and promoted an image of Francis that, while popular, is closer to fairy tale than to historical reality. The famous *Fioretti* or *Little Flowers of Saint Francis* provides probably the best-known collection of stories about Francis.

Not too many people, though, know that Francis left a few of his own writings—even some autographs—that members of his religious family have preserved and copied. While reading and meditating on Francis' words, some find themselves struck as by lightning; others "catch the virus" and are permanently infected by this man from Assisi. The latter happened to Thaddée Matura. It is the Francis of his writings that has attracted him. In the introduction of one of his major works, *Francis of Assisi: The Message in His Writings,* he wrote: "I have always felt drawn more to Francis' own writings.… From the beginning of my life as a Franciscan, I was fascinated by the lyrical nature of the writings, their quasi-liturgical style, and their aura of mysticism."

Francis of Assisi's writings are the writings of a passionate disciple of Jesus Christ. They literally distill the marrow of the gospel: love of God, love and care for neighbor—particularly the poor, the weak and the outcast—love and respect of creation. "Seek first the reign of

God and God's justice," writes Francis, quoting Matthew 6:33.

Thaddée Matura brings a rich personal history to his scholarly work. Originally from Poland, as a teenager Thaddée and his family moved to Canada where he later joined the Order of Friars Minor in the province of St. Joseph, Canada. He studied theology and Sacred Scriptures in Rome and in Jerusalem. For several years he was a member of the Franciscan fraternity in Taizé, France. Since the seventies Thaddée has lived in Provence, southern France. He has also traveled worldwide to give lectures and retreats. Over all those years Thaddée Matura has contributed many books and articles focused on Francis of Assisi and his evangelical way of life, as well as on the gospel itself. Unfortunately, only a few have been published in English, but they are significant. Allow me only to mention *The Gospel Life of Francis of Assisi Today* (Franciscan Press, 1980), *Gospel Radicalism: The Hard Sayings of Jesus* (Gill & Macmillan, 1984), *A Dwelling Place for the Most High* (Franciscan Press, 1998), and *Francis of Assisi: The Message in His Writings* (Franciscan Institute Publications, second edition, 2004), quoted above.

And now Thaddée Matura gives us *Francis of Assisi: Writer and Spiritual Master*, which was first published in French in the year 2000. Since we have enjoyed one another's friendship for some thirty years, Thaddée sent me a copy of it with his Christmas card that year, characterizing the book as "a kind of simple summary of many studies, of reflections and of experience, a kind of testament."

It is a little book. I have always loved little books. Maybe it is because of their portability: you can carry them with you. Big books will always wait on their shelves for your return: they know you cannot carry them away with you. But little books can accompany you, if not by their material pages, definitely by their contents if they are subtle enough to reach your heart. In the end only few things are necessary. That is exactly what Francis of Assisi understood, and Thaddée Matura in this little book, passes on to us.

Jean François Godet-Calogeras
The Franciscan Institute
St. Bonaventure University

PREFACE

Great theologians and holy men in the early church, such as Irenaeus, Origen and Augustine, as well as the doctors in the Middle Ages, such as Thomas Aquinas, Bonaventure and John Duns Scotus, have left us with numerous and important writings, which occupy a great deal of space in libraries. Yet, for all these texts that were written by these great masters, we do not have one autographed and handwritten version.

In the thirteenth century a layperson possessing only basic alphabetical skills (which meant knowing how to write and read Latin, the official language of the time) did not only leave a certain number of writings behind, but he also left behind something extremely rare for the period—two brief handwritten texts on pieces of parchment. This man is Francis of Assisi, little known as a writer. Without any educational background, nonetheless, he was able and loved to write or have others write for him. He insisted on the preservation of what he wrote, and he called for the transmission, knowledge and putting into practice of his writings. He was convinced of the power of the Word of God, which he had received in faith and to which he had oriented his life. The necessity of transmitting this belief into writing for everyone of every generation was a mission for him.

The book at hand wants to be at the service and as a prolongation of this mission.

PART ONE

FRANCIS OF ASSISI AS A WRITER AND SPIRITUAL MASTER

Is there such a thing as a Franciscan spiritual path? No one would hesitate to respond to this question in the affirmative. Without even attempting to define this path, this "spirituality," or even trying to describe it, we need only to observe the fact that for more than seven centuries, a great number of men and women of every category and social class have embraced the way of gospel Christian life, which was initially developed by Francis of Assisi. There exists a certain manner of perceiving and sensing reality, as well as practicing the promises and the demands of the Good News (the Gospels), that characterizes this path and those who are committed to it. This Franciscan sensibility, we can affirm without exaggeration, has made its mark and continues to influence the life of the entire church, for a Christian spirituality never has the monopoly over any single group.

When the time comes, however, to specify and to clarify what constitutes the originality of Franciscan spirituality within the church and alongside other spiritual currents, things are less clear. Recently in Milan, I needed to find an Italian book on Franciscan spirituality. I went to what I believed to be the best religious bookstore in the city located next to the front of the cathedral (the *Duomo*). I went directly to the "Spirituality" section that is extensive and well supplied. One could find everything there: the Fathers of the Desert; monastic spirituality in general and Cistercian spirituality in particular; Carmelite spirituality with its Thérèse and Teresa, John of the Cross and Edith Stein; Ignatian spirituality; the writings of the mystics.... But I found nothing there with the "Franciscan" label. To find it, I was told, I needed to go to the shelf entitled "Lives of the Saints." There, indeed, under this label I found a fairly large number of biographies almost exclusively of Francis and some editions of his writings.

This experience, often repeated while visiting religious bookstores, is cause for reflection and raises some questions. Why, contrary to all the other Christian spiritualities, which have also been given birth by illustrious figures, does Franciscan spirituality seem to be the only one that refers to itself through the life of its founder (Francis) and even identifies itself in some way with him? A second question is: after Francis, are there other figures, other movements? What is their relationship to the Franciscan spiritual current? Is there, then, one or several Franciscan spiritualities?

As far as I am concerned, Francis is indeed at the origin of Franciscan spirituality in both his written message and by his life, which sheds light on his message. The spiritual current that springs from his experience was developed, enriched and sometimes lost its vitality through the centuries. Other figures left their mark on it: Clare of Assisi, Brother Giles, Bonaventure, John Duns Scotus, Angela of Foligno, Jacopone da Todi and, in the fifteenth and sixteenth centuries, Henry of Herp (Harpius), Osuna, Benet of Canfield and so many others.

We can and must make the distinction between the *spirituality of Francis* and *Franciscan spirituality*, just as we distinguish the source of the river that flows from it. As for the *Franciscan spirituality*, we are still far from having a comprehensive view; so abundant is the material available and yet so little explored. The Italian collection, *Mistici Francescani*, and its Spanish equivalent, intends to fill this gap by the publication, in a dozen volumes, of texts stretching from the thirteenth century to the contemporary era. Recently (1998), Bernard McGinn, an American scholar of Western Christian mysticism, presented a remarkable and thorough synthesis of the Franciscan spiritual tradition of the thirteenth century in the third volume of his great work, *The Presence of God: A History of Western Christian Mysticism: The Flowering of Mysticism*.

As far as the spiritual path that is distinctive to Francis himself, it is the countless biographies, the record of the facts and deeds about him that, as it has just been said, intend and claim to introduce us to it. It is undeniable that these biographies of Francis reveal something of his vision of God and of how he, Francis, understood the human condition. The fact remains that what we have at hand is the personal journey characteristic of a particular figure, and, moreover, one that is subject to the interpretation of his biographers.

CHAPTER ONE

FRANCIS AS WRITER AND SPIRITUAL MASTER

We must change our approach, and without neglecting the light brought to it by Francis' singular destiny, question closely and directly the message which he has left us. For Francis has left us a written message, one addressed to his contemporaries, to be sure, but also and very explicitly one addressed to men and women of every era. This message does not set forward his personal example—Francis is not the center but the servant; what he does is simply lay out a path for us, one sustained by the Gospels and available to all believers. To speak of Francis, however, as a writer and a spiritual master is surprising. Isn't he someone who eludes the usual categories? Isn't he someone without scholarly training, who was hardly able to read and write Latin (the official language of the time)? And yet, from this man, who described himself as ignorant and without learning, textual critics have retained some thirty written pieces—of varying length—which form an anthology of some one hundred and fifty pages. Two precious documents have even been retained, which contain his handwriting on small parchments.

This anthology, which contains several literary genres (poems, legislative texts and short prayers), is nonetheless very unified in its style, and, above all, in its content. The writings are not disassociated pieces. We find a powerful personality behind them. With very simple means they succeed in aptly suggesting the basic realities that make up the life of a man or a woman receiving the gospel message into daily existence.

Strangely enough, down through the centuries, this message has not been taken into account as it deserves. Conserved piously and transmitted, Francis' texts by themselves were not taken into serious consideration as the basic and main source of his spiritual vision until the past fifty years.

These writings do not say much about Francis himself, but invite us to see how he conceived God and the Christian journey. With these writings as my foundation, I wish to propose here a comprehensive and synthetic vision of the spiritual path that Francis discovered in the Gospels and which he proposed for all to follow.

To facilitate the understanding of the discourse that follows and to situate it within a larger perspective, I precede it with a few considerations on the theology and the vision of the human condition such as can be deduced from Francis' writings, which form the basic framework of this essay.[1]

NOTES

[1] For those who would like a deeper and a more elaborate study of Francis' vision, I would like to refer them to: Thaddée Matura, O.F.M., *Francis of Assisi: The Message in His Writings*, trans. by Paul Barrett, O.F.M. Cap., (New York:

Franciscan Institute Publications, 1997). For something simpler and more meditative: Thaddée Matura, O.F.M, *A Dwelling Place for the Most High, Meditations with Francis of Assisi,* trans. by Paul Lachance, O.F.M., (Quincy, Ill.: Franciscan Press, 1999).

CHAPTER TWO

FRANCIS' THEOLOGY AND ANTHROPOLOGY

A sense of timelessness immediately emerges in Francis' writings. Not only is there scarcely any mention of Francis himself, there is no mention of the turmoil of the early thirteenth century, the period of time in which he wrote. Beyond a certain number of concrete attitudes proposed to Christians and to the brotherhood (radical poverty, work, mendicancy), which share the common viewpoint of the time, it is always the deep roots of these attitudes which are the focus. These texts are evangelical in the sense that, like the Gospels, they touch something eternal and permanent in the human condition: the misery of the human condition, yet a humanity loved by God and called upon to live life to its fullest. In other words, Francis' writings are essentially spiritual writings which reveal to humans the face of God, as well as their own, and invite them to follow the footprints of Christ in poverty and inner gladness.

What follows are the major traits of the spiritual vision underlying these writings.

The central place is given to the mystery of God the Father. Almost all the prayers are addressed to him, and three extraordinary texts, *Earlier Rule*, *Prayer Inspired by Our Father* and *The Praises of God*, try to say something of his being, his greatness and majesty as well as his nearness.[1]

The vision that Francis has of God is definitely Trinitarian, and, on this point, a correction is called for in regard to the oft-repeated affirmation that his spirituality was Christocentric, a Christocentrism strongly focused on the earthly life of Jesus (his cross and crib). Certainly, the role of the Lord Jesus Christ is also central, but his example and above all, his Word (the latter more emphasized than the former) always lead us to the Father. The spiritual experience, which Francis sings about, and the emotional tremor that can be perceived when he does so, are mainly concerned with the divine mystery of the Father. This Trinitarian equilibrium is admirably presented in the Prayer of Thanksgiving in Chapter Twenty-Three of the *First Rule*. It is the Father, along with his only Son and the Holy Spirit, who creates, redeems and brings the world to fulfillment of which men and women, created according to God's image, are the summit.

Men and women are never separable from God. Made to be at the highest level of creation, they have become, through their own fault, beings full of wretchedness. At the risk of upsetting contemporary sensitivity, Francis mercilessly stresses their state of corruption, their egocentricity and their sin. But ultimately this only serves to highlight the unconditional love of God, who is infatuated with those in wretchedness, ungrateful and evil as they are, and who is nothing but kind to them. With a very perceptive psychology, Francis makes a thorough search for and exposes, especially in the *Admonitions*, the regressions and the ruses of the egoistic self and calls for an acknowledgment of this wretched state, a dispossession of this self and ultimately fraternal service. These texts constitute a veritable charter of the essence of radical spiritual poverty.

Men and women once emptied and liberated from their egoistic selves can live the spirit of the Beatitudes and find perfect joy in trials and suffering. And when they have the Spirit of the Lord within themselves, they become truly free, and able to see clearly, commit themselves to the gospel journey and attain a high level of spiritual experience—as is described in the *Second Letter to the Faithful* (cf. *Francis of Assisi: The Saint, Volume 1*, p. 48–56).

Among Francis' writings, this letter is the one that comes closest to being an organic treatise of the spiritual life. It presents a complete spiritual itinerary: its ecclesial and sacramental components and its demands for the love of God and neighbor. Far from being simply a moral guide, it bases Christian life on the mystery of Christ, Word of the Father—his Incarnation, his Passion and his Eucharist. The end result of this itinerary is the entrance, in this life, into a communion with the Trinity.

If the writings destined for the fraternity (*Rules, Testament*) concern themselves, on many matters, with the concrete expression— a very flexible one to be sure—of fraternal life, they also very strongly point to their supreme objective: emptying the false self (ambition, pride, envy and a judgmental spirit) and desiring above all else to have in oneself the Spirit of the Lord (devoting oneself to prayer with a pure heart, living in humility, patience and love of those who do not love us). (Cf. *Later Rule* 10, v. 7–10.)

In technical terms one could say that Francis has a solid theology and anthropology rooted in Scripture and presented with simplicity and sobriety.

Other traits can be determined: the role of Mary; Francis' conception of the church, authority and the world; the way one behaves in the midst of others; the demands of poverty; the place of nature; and a poetic approach Francis sometimes rhetorically utilized. One notices that the main source, very explicitly emphasized wherein Francis finds his inspiration as well as the theological and spiritual content of the themes of his spirituality, is Scripture of both the Old and New Covenant, mediated by the liturgy. Some texts are but a long chain of quotations judiciously chosen and forming a coherent whole.

These few lines are sufficient to reveal in Francis a true spiritual master of a special genre since he is a layperson without any school learning. Apart from a few Fathers of the Desert whose sayings have been reported to us—the so-called *apophtegma*—(many of whom did not have a theological culture) there is no masculine figure—or writer—of this type in the Christian tradition.

Francis is closer to certain feminine personalities of the Middle Ages, such as Angela of Foligno or Catherine of Siena—both unlettered—and in our day Thérèse of Lisieux, who possessed a more modest theological and biblical baggage than Augustine, Bernard or John of the Cross, who were learned and scholarly. But because he is simple, because he speaks to us of the Gospels without being too marked by the bearings of a particular epoch and its culture, Francis' message reaches us more easily than a figure with an imposing stature; he comes across to us as immediate and contemporary.

Questions for Reflection

1. What is the spiritual Franciscan path based upon? What are its primary references—the figure and the life of Francis or his written message?

2. Can one and should one distinguish between the two?

3. Upon what do you base your own spiritual path? How does this compare with the Franciscan path?

NOTES

[1] Translations from and references to the writings of Saint Francis are taken from *The Saint, Francis of Assisi: Early Documents*, *Volume 1*, edited by Regis Armstrong, J. A. Wayne Hellmann and William Short (New York: New City Press, 1999).

PART TWO

THE MAIN LINES
OF THE SPIRITUALITY
OF THE WRITINGS

CHAPTER THREE

WHAT IS SPIRITUALITY?

In order to speak accurately about Franciscan spirituality it is necessary to specify its relationship to Christian spirituality in general, as well as with the various spiritual currents within Christianity.

Christian spirituality consists of a comprehensive vision of all of reality: God, the human condition and the way in which men and women participate in the world and find expression in a particular way of life. This vision and this way of life come from and find their basis in the manifestation of God whose summit is the coming into flesh of the Son, the Word of the Father and the universal outpouring of the breath of God, the Spirit of holiness. Christian spirituality is a life in the Spirit; a gift of God. It is a vision and an experience to which we have access through faith, the sacraments and personal effort. It is based on the totality of revelation contained in the Scriptures and the tradition of the church and finds its expression in the new life produced in us by the Spirit.

THE DIFFERENT SPIRITUALITIES

Christian spirituality is meant to be all-encompassing. We need to notice, however, that in the past as well as in the present, there exists numerous spiritualities. Thus one can find patristic, monastic, Carmelite or Ignatian spiritualities, to name a few. What does this multiplicity mean? How is each related to the gospel of Christ and how can each be justified with its unique foundation? Does each form of spirituality add something? Is there a hierarchy among them or a different equilibrium? These are all questions that deserve to be asked and answered.

The spiritual currents that appear throughout history are only meant to be a rediscovery of the inexhaustible riches of the Christian spiritual treasury. At the onset, there is almost always a figure who, awakened by the Spirit, hears as if it were for the first time, the Word which calls for the fulfillment of the life that was announced and inaugurated by the Lord. Whether it be Anthony, the father of monastic life; Augustine, the doctor and the mystic; Bernard; Ignatius of Loyola; or Teresa of Avila, each wants to assume personally the totality of the message in its internal hierarchy and equilibrium. They impregnate themselves with it, strive to live it out: in both who they are and in what they usually transmit by their writings, they devise a spiritual path—a spirituality—for others.

We then can question, and rightly so, the originality of such spiritualities. If they are but the rediscovery of and the serious undertaking of the basic Christian vision, in what way then are they different, original? If they leave important elements by the wayside or introduce others that have no relationship with the gospel or even contradict it, can they still be called Christian spiritualities? And, if they insist on just a few points of the Christian heritage, do they throw it off balance and become, at best, only a devotion, which is something completely different than a spirituality?

Also, or so it seems, the originality of the shape of a spirituality cannot exist only in a particular element. If it wishes to be fully Christian it owes to itself to take in all the riches, the harmony and the equilibrium of the totality. One cannot say that the center of such a spirituality is the liturgy, poverty or prayer. There can be no other center but God the Father, Christ and the Holy Spirit who call men and women to enter into communion with its overflowing life.

The originality consists, rather, in a certain sensibility which is specific to the founding figure and which makes him or her present the totality of the Christian vision according to a special coherence. In other words, the constitutive elements of an authentic spirituality can only always remain the same; only in how it is arranged, presented and put together can it be considered different. An image of a floral arrangement can illustrate this abstract affirmation. With a dozen identical flowers entrusted to several artists, there will be as many different flower arrangements as there are artists.

THE SPIRITUALITY OF FRANCIS OF ASSISI

We can now situate Franciscan spirituality with greater facility in its initial emergence as the vision and personal experience of Francis. As with so many other witnesses of God before and after him, Francis rediscovers by circuitous approaches and by and above all a revelation from God of what is the "*vita evangelii Jesu Christi*," a life that the gospel of Christ proclaims and brings to the world. Francis, layperson without a clerical culture who has the heart of the poor and the little ones, receives from the "Father, the Lord of heaven and earth," the full revelation of the mystery of God and of his love for the world and for all men and women. He receives it into his life, he lives from it and— this is a paradox for someone who calls himself "ignorant and an idiot"—he leaves behind writings which, without any pretense of wanting to create a synthesis, provide a vision which is sufficiently ample, at any rate, deep, of what we can call a spiritual path, a spirituality. What will be presented in what follows is based not on the narratives of the life of Francis, which describe and interpret it, but on the very writings of Francis himself. The difference is a big one because in the biographies it is the figure of Francis, what he said and did, that predominates while the center of Francis' writings is God, men and women and the path that leads from one to the other.

At the beginning a distinction was made between the spirituality of Francis and Franciscan spirituality; we must now specify what this means. The spirituality of Francis is based on his experience and his personal vision, and it is his writings that are the most faithful, if not the most complete, expression of it. This experience and this vision have been received, understood and lived differently by those who have wanted to follow this way. They have brought additions to it, developments, different emphases and at times omissions —throughout the centuries. These outgrowths, these evolutions, this influence due to life itself and also due to the presence of powerful personalities are what form the great river of Franciscan spirituality. But, as it has been said at the beginning, what will be presented here is the source, Francis' very own vision. This does not mean that these developments and these evolutions did not have any meaning in the past or do not have any for today; but to reconnect with the freshness and the vigor of the Franciscan spiritual current, one must return to the source. The initial and original blossoming will restore the purity of the waters of the river, allow us to eliminate deviations, and will infuse a new dynamism to Franciscan spirituality.

Our Approach

Now that we have been given the possibility of seeing what is at issue, it is time to speak about the spirituality of Francis. We must enter into the subject matter and present the main lines of this spirituality, using, if possible, Francis' own words and expressions. At the center of Francis' vision, we find the mystery of God in its Trinitarian dimension: the Father as source and fulfillment of all that is, the Word of the Father who has taken on the flesh of our humanity and our fragility, and the Spirit Paraclete who never ceases to act in us. The first part of our treatise will be dedicated to God "whom no one is worthy of naming," to whom the heart of humanity must always be turned in adoration and thanksgiving, the one who is infinitely delectable and above all desirable.

What follows will be the vision, one full of contrasts, of the human condition, of men and women made in the image of God, a condition of incomparable elevation and at the same time one of inexhaustible misery, a condition considered both in the individual and as member of the human and ecclesial community.

After what could be called the theology and anthropology of Francis, we will attempt to describe the Christian path that is proposed for men and women. It is a path of love and adoration of God, of communion with the church, of love and humble service to all men and women as brothers and sisters and of a radical poverty of being and material expression, in order to walk in the footsteps of Christ and through that path to reach fulfillment in happiness.

Questions for Reflection

1. How would you define "spirituality" or "the spiritual life" of a Christian? Do you think spirituality concerns our relationship with God (contemplation, union with God, prayer, etc.), or does it entail all the aspects of one's life, one's rapport with self, neighbor, God?

2. What aspect of the spiritual life is most prominent in your own life?

3. What do you think you need to do to establish a better balance in your spiritual life? How will you go about achieving this balance?

CHAPTER FOUR

FRANCIS' VISION: A TRINITARIAN GOD

THE PRIMACY OF "THE FATHER MOST HOLY"

All powerful, most holy,
Almighty and supreme God,
Holy and just Father,
Lord King of heaven and earth
we thank You for Yourself
for through Your holy will
and through Your only Son
with the Holy Spirit
You have created everything spiritual and corporal
and, after making us in Your own image and likeness,
You placed us in Paradise.

Through our own fault we fell.

We thank You
for as through Your Son You created us,
so through Your holy love

with which You loved us
You brought about His birth
As true God and true man
by the glorious, ever-virgin, most blessed, holy Mary
and You willed to redeem us captives
through His cross and blood and death.

We thank You
for Your Son Himself will come again
in the glory of His majesty
to send into the eternal fire
the wicked ones
who have not done penance
and have not known You
and to say to all those
who have known You, adored You and served You in penance:
"Come, you blessed of my Father,
receive the kingdom prepared for you
from the beginning of the world."

Because all of us, wretches and sinners,
are not worthy to pronounce Your name,
we humbly ask
our Lord Jesus Christ,
Your beloved Son,
in Whom You were well pleased,
together with the Holy Spirit,
the Paraclete,
to give You thanks,
for everything
as it pleases You and Him,
Who always satisfies You in everything,
Through Whom You have done so much for us.
Alleluia!

—"Prayer and Thanksgiving," *The Earlier Rule* 23[1]

At the center of Francis' vision, as attested to by very powerful texts, (*Admonitions 1*; *Earlier Rule 23*; *Second Letter to the Faithful, The Praises of God* and so many others) appears the one "whom no one can name." Francis writes of this reality with great reverence, and to indicate its unfathomable and ineffable mystery, he attributes to it more than eighty different names, as if to show that none of them are adequate to "define" it. This God-Father, to whom even the Son and the Spirit unceasingly give thanks, is supremely exalted: the Most High *par excellence*, "Exalted above all, sublime" and yet he makes himself so immanent and near. "Gentle, lovable, delightful, and totally desirable above all else,"[2] he is the source of absolute happiness for men and women, all "their riches to sufficiency."[3] Everyone is invited to "serve, love, honor and adore Him with a pure heart and mind"[4] and in the best way possible. The goal of the spiritual path is "By Your grace alone, we make our way to You, Most High"[5] and thus become his sons and daughters.

The Father holds the initiative for everything that is to take place. He is the one, along with the Son and the Holy Spirit, who created the world and humans according to his image: it is he who makes his Son to be born in the flesh, save us by his cross, and manifest him on the last day. It is to him that Jesus addresses his filial prayer in the fifteen psalms arranged by Francis; it is the Father again whom Francis invokes in almost all his prayers that he has left us. As in John's Gospel, of which Francis is strongly tributary, the Father occupies the only and unique place; he holds the primacy. This perspective, one that is so clear in Francis' writings, obliges us to revise a certain conception of the Christocentrism which is presented as being specific to Franciscan spirituality. To be sure, Christians that we are, we can but be "Christocentric" without forgetting, however, that Christ's way is centered on the Father.

"The Word of the Father, so worthy, so holy and glorious"

The most high Father made known from heaven through His holy angel Gabriel this Word of the Father—so worthy, so holy and glorious—in the womb of the holy and glorious Virgin Mary, from whose womb He received the flesh of our humanity and frailty. Though He was rich, He wished, together with the most Blessed Virgin, His mother, to choose poverty in the world beyond all else. And, as His Passion was near, He celebrated the Passover with His disciples and, taking bread, gave thanks, blessed and broke it, saying: *Take and eat: This is My body.* And taking the cup He said: *This is my Blood of the New Covenant which will be poured out for you and for many for the forgiveness of sins.* Then He prayed to his Father, saying: *Father, if it can be done, let this cup pass from me. And his sweat became as drops of blood falling on the ground.* Nevertheless, He placed His will in the will of His Father, saying: *Father, let Your will be done; not as I will, but as You will.* His Father's will was such that His blessed and glorious Son, Whom He gave to us and Who was born for us, should offer Himself through His own blood as a sacrifice and oblation on the altar of the cross: not for Himself through Whom all things were made, but for our sins, leaving us an example that we might follow His footprints.

—*Second Letter to the Faithful*[6]

"Through the holy love with which He loved us,"[7] the Father gave us his Son and made him to be born in the glorious and poor Virgin Mary. This Son, "so worthy, holy and glorious," took on the flesh of our humanity and fragility, and together with His Mother, chose poverty. He is the way that leads us to the Father[8] and we remember the love which he manifested to us is to be our daily bread.[9]

Francis has a very accurate theological vision of the mystery of Christ. Christ is "true God and true man."[10] He is the Lord of the universe, equal to the Father, God and Son of God. Upon hearing his name, Lord Jesus Christ, Son of the Most High, one must "adore, with fear and reverence, *prostrate on the ground*."[11] When it concerns Christ's humanity, Francis will stress two moments of his human itinerary: his coming into flesh, as the mystery of his poverty and divine humiliation; and his saving Passion and death as the manifestation of the love he had for us.[12] It is important to point out that even if the teachings of Jesus, his words, are quoted abundantly, very little is written about the earthly life of Jesus. Similarly, when the subject is the Passion, the stress is on the interior attitudes of Jesus—his trust-filled prayer and his self-donation to the Father—rather than on its outer expression such as the offenses and the contempt he suffered, the cross, and so forth.

CHRIST'S PRESENCE TODAY

The mystery of Christ unfolded in history—Incarnation, glorious Passion, Resurrection—and yet it is always present and reaches us in our everyday reality. "The Good Shepherd," writes Francis, quoting John's Gospel, who takes care of us after having given his life for us, is always with us until the end of time. Furthermore, we must turn toward him; bind ourselves to him in order to create a true fraternal community.[13] Even if his presentation is not a systematic one, Francis, with penetrating intuition, points out the four ways by which Christ is present to us today.

He is first of all present in the community assembled in his name. "*Wherever two or three are gathered together in my name, there I am in the midst of them.*"[14] We dwell in Him, and His *words—spirit and life—* dwell in us and give us life. His words—his gospel message—which are also life-giving and dynamic words of the Spirit[15] and whose infinite riches must be discovered in gladness and joy,[16] save us at the same time as the sacrament of the Body and the Blood of Christ.[17] They are, by this very fact, the second location of the Lord's presence. By making an effort to be open to his words, to understand them spiritually, and to live them out, we encounter and honor the Lord himself.[18]

The Eucharist—celebration and communion—is the privileged moment for the actualization of Christ and his mystery. The eucharistic celebration, the rite along with the material elements of bread and wine, is the only presence available to our senses of Jesus Christ, incarnate, dead and risen. The Son of God abases himself and is made available to our faith each day just as when he incarnated himself. In these elements so ordinary as to be banal, he comes to us daily under humble appearances. His presence in the sacrament manifests his humility—his kenosis—as well as that of the Father "who accepts each day that His unique Son comes down *from the bosom of the Father* upon the altar in the hands of a priest."[19] Francis never forgets that the one who humbles himself in the anonymity of the Eucharist is the Lord of the universe, God and Son of God, no longer mortal but living and glorified for eternity.[20]

Finally, today, as in his great eucharistic prayer on the night of his Passion (John 17), Christ continues revealing the name of the Father to us as well as praying for us. This "priestly" prayer of Christ is quoted three times in Francis' writings. He retains the demands in our favor that the Son addresses to the Father: unity, joy, preservation from evil, knowledge of the love of God for us, and participation in the destiny of the Son and his glory.

THE PATHS FOR THE EXPERIENCE OF CHRIST

But how can one discover, beyond words and the material signs, the reality of the living Lord? How can one experience him?

This question is raised in the first *Admonition*, which is a brief veritable treatise of spiritual knowledge. A path is traced: it begins with the knowledge of the Son "according to the Spirit and divinity" to reach, through the Spirit who dwells in the faithful, the invisible Father. We begin first of all by approaching what was or remains visible of Christ: humanity, flesh, sacrament—in other words, what one can see and grasp. But this is only the surface; to enter into the reality, we must allow ourselves to be led by the Spirit who grants us "spiritual eyes." We are then introduced to the very interior of Christ and he reveals to us, by his divine and human nature simultaneously, the face of the Father. The path of the knowledge of Christ leads us, in the Spirit, to attain the depths of the Father.

The summit of spiritual experience is admirably described in the text addressed not to the brothers, but to Christians living in the world.[21] When they pursue the gospel path with tenacity, the Spirit of the Lord will rest upon them and will make a home and a dwelling place within them. They will then share in the Trinitarian communion: the Spirit makes of them sons and daughters of the celestial Father; spouses, brothers and mothers of Jesus Christ, Son of the Father. They are by that very fact brothers and sisters of Jesus; even more, they become spouses—a mystical theme *par excellence*—when the Spirit unites the faithful soul to Christ. By their faith and their works, they become mothers of Christ, carrying him in their hearts and giving birth to him for the sake of the world. The "mysticism" of Francis boldly proposed for all believers, is to be sure Christocentric, but always within a Trinitarian perspective; it is the Spirit who makes of us sons and daughters of the Father, and brothers, spouses and mothers of Jesus.

The Spirit Paraclete

> And *the Spirit of the Lord will rest upon* all those men and women who have done and persevered in these things and it will make a home and a *dwelling place in them*. And they will be the children of the heavenly Father, Whose works they do. And they are spouses, brothers and mothers of our Lord Jesus Christ. We are spouses when the faithful soul is united by the Holy Spirit to our Lord Jesus Christ. We are brothers, moreover, when we do the will of His Father Who is in heaven; mothers when we carry Him in our heart and body through love and a pure and sincere conscience; and give Him birth through a holy activity, which must shine before others by example.
>
> —*The Second Letter to the Faithful*[22]

When in his principal texts Francis sketches a comprehensive vision of God the Father and his work, one always finds the presence of the Spirit next to and adjacent to the Son. The Spirit, the holy one, the Paraclete, the defender and consoler, is often called "the Spirit of the Lord" as if to stress the links to the Father and the Son. Fire, light, breath, inspiration, gratuitous gift of God and Spirit is above all "the Holy love" with which the Father loves us. It is to the Spirit primarily that we can apply the qualities that Francis attributes to God: *tender, modest, beloved, friendly, accessible, innocent, exquisite, lovable, delectable, desirable.*

However, the Spirit being what is deepest and most mysterious in God, even these attempts at description fall short. Spirit is what is inexpressible in God. Rather than stammer a few words that fall short of describing his being, Francis will indicate throughout his writings the dynamism of the Spirit, the activities or, as he calls them, his *operations.*

The Operations of the Spirit

These operations of the Spirit are multiple and varied; they are at work in God as well as in the men and women in whom the Spirit dwells. We must be attentive to what Francis says of the Spirit; once we understand what he means and allow the Spirit to act in us, we learn the essence of what he means by "the spiritual life" as well as the essence of Franciscan "spirituality."

The Spirit, Saint Paul tells us, probes the depths of God (the Father). He is the only one who knows them (1 Corinthians 2:10–11). Francis catches a glimpse of the role of the Spirit within God. God is Spirit, no one has ever seen God, and one can only know him in the Spirit.[23] Thus it is the Spirit who sees God, who represents in some way the visibility of God and then communicates it to those on whom he finds rest. Moreover, the Spirit is the one who makes the Word of God come alive; the words of Christ himself, the Word of the Father, are equally words of the Spirit and therefore possess a dynamic life.[24] And with the Son, coming from and dependent on the Father as he is himself, the Spirit is the one who celebrates and is the cantor of the Father from whom he emerges.[25]

What occurs in the perpetual outpouring from within the Trinity finds expression in the history of salvation. With the Father, who has the initiative, the Spirit and the Son intervene in creation, in the redemptive Incarnation[26] and are active in the celebration of the Eucharist.[27]

As for the life of the faithful believer, his "operations" are constantly animated by the energies of the Spirit. The believer is born again in the water and by the Spirit,[28] and it is the Spirit that makes the believer acknowledge and confess the divinity of Christ.[29] Without him it is impossible "to see and to believe, according to the Spirit and the divinity, that the body and the blood of Christ is in the Eucharist, and above all to receive him in truth," for, as Francis writes strongly, "it is the Spirit which dwells in the faithful who receives these most holy mysteries."[30]

The Spirit's main activity in humans, so to speak, is the "prayer of a pure heart." According to Jesus' words, which Francis quotes three times, one must adore the Father *in Spirit and in truth* (John 5:23–24). The Spirit, the only true adorer of the Father, who alone probes the depths "with fearsome awe," teaches men and women what adoration means. He is, according to Francis' expression, the "Spirit of holy prayer and devotion," that is to say the one who stirs the hearts of men and women to desire and to search for God and teaches them true spiritual worship which consists in obedience and service (devotion).[31] Also, we must desire the Spirit's presence more than anything else and leave room for his activity in us. The first fruit of his operation will be the prayer of a pure heart, then humility, patience and at its summit, the love of enemies.[32] For it is the work of the Spirit to push love to its absolute limits.[33]

The Spirit accompanies men and women on their spiritual journey that starts with the acknowledgment of our miserable state, continues with the discovery of the plan of God for us and culminates in how it is put into action. The intervention of the Spirit is necessary to enable us to follow the footsteps of Jesus, the Beloved Son, and attain the Father, the Most High and thus share in the glorious life of the Trinity. Only the Spirit can accomplish that which we are incapable of achieving through our own efforts and our own strength: the purification of the ambiguities that dwell in us, the light of a complete knowledge and, finally, a love set ablaze. Thus one must pray to be "interiorly purified, interiorly illuminated and set ablaze by the fire of the Spirit."[34]

Already in this life for the faithful who follow the path of the gospel, the fulfillment of the work of the Spirit occurs when he rests upon the faithful and they are introduced to the intimacy of the Father and the Son. This experience which is proposed for all—and which is realized first of all and fully so in Mary[35] as well as in the Poor Sisters of Saint Clare[36] is in some way the summit of the operations of the Paraclete. As in John's Gospel, which ascribes to the Father and the Son, "we will come to them and make our home with them" (John 14:23). Francis ascribes first of all to the Spirit. When the latter rests upon the faithful, as he did on the messianic figure in Isaiah (11:2), on Jesus at his baptism (John 1:32) and on those who suffer (1 Peter 4:1), he makes a home and a dwelling place and opens access to the Trinitarian life. In a daring and innovative way, Francis presents the role of the Spirit in mystical union under a nuptial form. The Spirit is the bond that unites the faithful soul to Christ in order to enable it to become a spouse: and moreover, he is the spouse of the Virgin Mary and also of the Poor Sisters.

One can now better understand the frequency with which Francis uses terms such as "spiritual" and "spiritually." According to Francis, someone is spiritual when one is under the influence of the Spirit and follows his promptings. To act spiritually means to discern, to judge according to the Spirit, in order then to incarnate it in one's daily life.

Such is the vision, traced in broad strokes, which Francis has of the Father Most High, his Beloved Son and the most Holy Paraclete[37]—a vision that inspired him and on which his life was based and on which ours must also be based.

Questions for Reflection

1. The vision that Francis has of God is decidedly Trinitarian. The reading of Francis' texts invites us to rediscover the true dimension of the divine communion of the Father-Son-Spirit. What are the implications of this Trinitarian vision for your life?

2. Do you share a relationship with each of the persons of the Trinity? If so, what is it?

3. Which person of the Trinity appeals to you most? Why?

NOTES

[1] *Francis of Assisi, Vol. 1, Earlier Rule 23*, vv. 1–5, pp. 81–83.

[2] *Ibid., Earlier Rule 23,* v. 11, pp. 85–86.

[3] *Ibid., The Praises of God*, v. 4, p. 109.

[4] *Ibid., Earlier Rule 22,* v. 26 p. 80.

[5] *Ibid., Letter to the Entire Order*, v. 52, p. 121.

[6] *Ibid., Second Letter to the Faithful,* vv. 4–13, p. 46.

[7] *Ibid., Earlier Rule 23,* v. 3, p. 81.

[8] *Ibid., Admonitions 1,* v. 1, p. 128.

[9] *Ibid., Prayer Inspired by Our Father,* v. 6, p. 159.

[10] *Ibid., Earlier Rule 22,* vv. 33–35, pp. 80–81.

[11] *Ibid., A Letter to the Entire Order*, v. 4, p. 116.

[12] *Ibid., Prayer Inspired by Our Father,* v. 6, p. 159.

[13] *Ibid., Earlier Rule 22,* vv. 33–35, pp. 80–81.

[14] *Ibid.,* p. 81.

[15] *Ibid., Second Letter to the Faithful,* v. 3, p. 46.

[16] *Ibid., Admonitions 20*, vv. 1–2, p. 135.

[17] *Ibid., Second Letter to the Faithful,* v. 34, p. 47.

[18] *Ibid., A Letter to the Entire Order,* v. 36, p. 119.

[19] *Ibid., Admonitions 1*, vv. 17–18, 129.

[20] *Ibid., A Letter to the Entire Order*, v. 22, p. 118.

[21] *Ibid., Second Letter to the Faithful,* vv. 48–53, pp. 48–49.

[22] *Ibid., Second Letter to the Faithful,* vv. 48–53, pp. 48–49.

[23] *Ibid., Admonitions 1*, v. 6, 128.

[24] *Ibid., Second Letter to the Faithful,* v. 3, p. 45.

[25] *Ibid., Earlier Rule 23,* vv. 5–6, pp. 82–83.

[26] *Ibid., Earlier Rule 23,* v. 1, p. 81.

[27] *Ibid., A Letter to the Entire Order*, v. 33, p. 119.

[28] *Ibid., Earlier Rule 16,* v. 7, p. 74.

[29] *Ibid., Admonitions 8*, v. 1, 132.

[30] *Ibid., Admonitions 1*, v. 12, 129.

[31] *Ibid., Later Rule 5,* v. 2, p. 102.

[32] *Ibid., Later Rule 10,* vv. 7–10, p. 105.

[33] *Ibid., Earlier Rule 5,* v. 13, p. 67.

[34] *Ibid., A Letter to the Entire Order*, vv. 50–52, pp. 120–121.

[35] *Ibid., Office of the Passion*, p. 139.

[36] Fragments from the *Rule of Saint Clare.*

[37] *Francis of Assisi, Vol. 1, The Testament,* v. 40, p. 124.

CHAPTER FIVE

WHO AM I? SO ADMIRABLE AND YET SO WOEFUL

The mystery of God, Father-Son-Spirit, is not only some far-off spectacle offered for our contemplation; it consists in an invitation to participate in the fullness of life and love: "The Lord *God* offers *Himself* to us as if we were His *children*,"[1] writes Francis citing Hebrews 12:7. Men and women are created by love to share in God's life. The important twenty-third chapter of the *Earlier Rule* synthesizes the vision that Francis has of God and the human condition, granting as much place to one as to the other. For Francis, if someone cannot imagine humankind without God, it is equally true that he cannot imagine God without humankind. His writings, even if in a fragmentary way, are very concerned with the human condition, and his vision of it is one full of contrasts. Humans are at once a mixture of admirable uniqueness and inexpressible misery. These are the two aspects of Francis' anthropology that we need to consider now. Thus we will be able to know better how admirable and yet how woeful is the condition of the ones whom God calls to communion with himself.

"...IN WHAT GREAT EXCELLENCE THE LORD GOD HAS PLACED YOU!"

> Consider, O human being, in what great excellence the Lord God has placed you, for He created and formed you to the image of His Beloved Son according to the body and to His likeness according to the Spirit. [2]

> ...Let us all love *the Lord God*
> Who has given and gives to each one of us
> our whole body, our whole soul, and our whole life
> Who has created, redeemed and will save us by His mercy alone. [3]

What enables men and women to exist is the result of the love that God wants to extend outside of himself. God is not egotistically centered on himself: "Because of himself and his holy will," he creates corporal and spiritual realities and, at their summit, men and women made "according to his image and his likeness." God loves men and women so much that he creates a body for them made in the image of his own Son, and destines them to the happiness of Paradise. Through creation he bestowed upon us and always bestows upon us "all our bodies, soul, and life." After the Fall, "because of the holy love with which He loved us," he snatched us from slavery and "did and does everything good for us and will save us by His mercy alone," even if we are "miserable and wretched, rotten and foul, ungrateful and evil ones."[4] According to Francis, the basis for the incomparable human dignity of men and women and the source of the values and dynamisms that spring from it lie in God's desire and dream that men and women become his partners.

These values, which constitute the human being and for which one must ceaselessly be thankful, are elementary and concrete, one could even say, "down to earth" realities. It is the fact that our body is made according to the image of the Son which gives value to the body and alters the image of the asceticism, the scorn of the body, which is often attributed to Francis: our soul—made into God's likeness and drawn to Him—is our life. The beauty of the body, intellectual capabilities, perceptiveness, knowledge, experience, spiritual charisms, in a word: "having," "power," "knowledge"[5]—all that is part of the makeup of men and women called to divine communion. To be sure, this makeup can be perverted if we appropriate it for ourselves and we rely only on it, but independently of the higher divine gifts, these are the first benefits that God generously bestows upon us.

Men and women are also abundantly provided for by powers, energies and capacities for action. A material body, obviously, but a body inhabited by the soul, principal of life, and endowed with a heart which is not, as is often the case for us, just a feeling, but rather, according to its rich biblical meaning, the deepest center of the person. The heart is accompanied by what Francis calls in Latin *mens,* and which we roughly translate by mental "intelligence of the heart." Thus endowed, men and women are capable of making use of and putting into action immense capacities. In a pressing invitation to love God, Francis enumerates, in a single sentence, as many as twelve of these capacities, adding expressions of his own to the biblical ones. Yes, each one of us must love God with the whole heart, soul and spirit, but this is not enough. We must add other interior capacities: strength, fortitude, understanding, powers, effort, affection, feelings, desire, wishes. After all this how could one accuse Francis of having a pessimistic anthropology?

If we are invited to such an outburst of energy, it is because we are capable of using it. Yes, as Francis repeats several times, "God does, says, or works good words and deeds in and through us." [6] To be sure, we must not appropriate them and glorify ourselves as if they were our own, yet the fact remains that these things exist and are visible. We are indeed called to do "much and even greater."[7] What is essential in this activity can be reduced to two dimensions: one is our essential objective, the experience of God, "to desire nothing else, want nothing else, let nothing else please and cause us delight except the only true God;"[8] and the other is the love of neighbor whom one must cherish as Jesus did. That is to say, love them with a love that is humble, concrete, similar to a motherly one, a love which extends itself to all our brothers and sisters even if they are "useless and are enemies."

The greatest nobility and dignity of human beings lies in the call that is made to them "to make their way to the Father Most High and to share in the life, rule, and glory which He enjoys with the Son and the Spirit."[9] An approach and a foretaste of this communal sharing is already experienced in this life through faith. To know that the Spirit rests upon us, to know that he dwells in us as in a temple, that he makes of us sons and daughters of the Father in heaven, brothers and sisters, spouse, and mothers of Jesus, even if it is still experienced in a darkness, of such is the fulfillment of the life of the Christian, sign and proof of the incomparable grandeur of this vocation. In the regimen of grace, what is lived today in the obscurity and the groping of faith will be unveiled in its plenitude when "our Father will make us come into His kingdom. There the clear vision, the perfect delights, the blessed companionship, the eternal enjoyment of who He is will become manifest."[10]

"WE CAN CLAIM AS OUR OWN ONLY OUR VICES AND OUR SINS"

> In the love that is God, therefore, I beg all my brothers—those who preach, pray, or work, cleric or lay—to strive to humble themselves in everything, not to boast or delight in themselves or inwardly exalt themselves because of the good words and deeds or, for that matter, because of any good that God sometimes says or does or works in and through them, in keeping with what the Lord says: *Do not rejoice because the spirits are subject to you*. We may know with certainty that nothing belongs to us except our vices and sins. We must rejoice, instead, when we fall *into various trials* and, in this world, suffer every kind of anguish or distress of soul and body for the sake of eternal life.[11]

After the positive and luminous side of the human condition, we are also presented, in violent contrast, with its shadowy side. When he focuses on the real status of the human condition in which we all find ourselves since "through our fault we have fallen,"[12] Francis, in order to describe it, uses strong expressions that we can hardly find acceptable or understandable, because they seem so merciless. "We have nothing of our own except our vices and our sins"[13] "…because, by our own fault, we are disgusting, miserable and opposed to good, yet prompt and inclined to evil."[14] The diabolical couplet "vices and sins" is almost commonplace in his writings and they appear twelve times.

In these expressions are we to understand a pessimistic anthropology of Augustinian origin pushed to an extreme and exaggerated, and also made worse by medieval rhetoric and Francis' personal experience? Or rather, aside from the language used, are they not a realistic appraisal and description of the human condition? Francis invents nothing; he is extremely sensitive to what the Lord says in the Gospel:

"For it is from within, from the human heart, that evil intentions come" (Mark 7:21). He quotes these words four times. Even if it is true that the adversary, the devil, wants the love of our Lord Jesus Christ taken away from us and tries to lodge himself in soiled hearts, he is not the one mainly responsible for evil; rather, we are the ones responsible for it.[15]

THE MANIFESTATIONS OF EVIL

There is an inveterate tendency toward evil "to delight," as Francis writes, "in vices and sins."[16] In his writings, which even if they do propose primarily a path to holiness and salvation, Francis does not hesitate to designate with precision the multiple manifestations of evil which threaten everyone, especially, perhaps, those who commit themselves to a life according to the Gospels. In the first place, indifference to and forgetfulness of God; even if "one has left the world," one can become, without being aware of it, deaf to God's word that no longer finds in us a fertile ground in which to grow.[17] The heart, which should be always turned toward the Lord by being attentive, alert and in prayer, can let itself be overtaken by worries, preoccupations and obstacles. And there is so much to be said about interpersonal relationships, always threatened as they are by quarrels, conflicts, negative criticisms, judgments, condemnations and above all by emotional upset and anger—all of which destroy interior and exterior peace as well as charity.[18] Greed and avarice, waywardness, hardness of heart,[19] and carnal lust are but part of a long list which demonstrates that Francis had no illusions about the human condition, and that he had a keen psychological awareness of it.

The most serious tendency to evil, however, does not occur in situations where evil is acknowledged as such. What one must beware of above all is the temptation to appropriate for oneself the good that belongs to God. We have already previously mentioned that the human person is abundantly endowed by God with gifts of all kinds, both material and spiritual. One must acknowledge the origin of these gifts, rejoice over them, promote them; but once this is done, one must "render" them, restore them to the One to whom they belong in an act of praise and thanksgiving. Those who consider themselves owners of what they have and of the good deeds and words that God accomplishes in them and by them rob God of the glory that belongs to him. They reiterate for themselves Adam's sin who wanted to be like God,[20] become a robber like Judas, [21] and take pride and exalt themselves in what does not belong to them. Moreover, not content with snatching for themselves what does not belong to them but to God, they become sad over the belongings of others, envy them and become jealous of them, thus becoming guilty of blasphemy, for by doing so they envy God himself.[22] We find ourselves here at the very heart of evil: the radical negation of true poverty which consists in acknowledging that all good comes from God and must be rendered back to him in thanksgiving.

It is not surprising that in speaking of what is involved in following the gospel (and in order to shed light on the seriousness of what is at stake for the ones who commit themselves to the path of faith), Francis also speaks of the possibility of refusing God and the merit of eternal punishment (hell). If this point is not a central, nor even an important one, in his vision, it is nonetheless present as an invitation to take extremely seriously the call to follow Christ.

Having reached the end of this anthropological survey, we need to take note of the human and gospel balance and realism of the perspective indicated by Francis. Now we can better understand the title we have given to this section: the admirableness and the woefulness of the human condition. It is an admirableness based on the incomprehensible love of the One who never ceases to do good for those "who are miserable and woeful, rotten and foul, ungrateful and evil ones."[23]

The Community of Saints and Sinners

> All of us lesser brothers, useless servants, humbly ask and beg those who wish to serve the Lord God within the holy Catholic and Apostolic church and all the following orders: priests, deacons, subdeacons, acolytes, exorcists, lectors, porters, and all clerics, all religious men and women, all penitents and youths, the poor and the needy, kings and princes, workers and farmers, servants and masters, all virgins, continent and married women, all laypeople, men and women, all children, adolescents, young and old, the healthy and the sick, all the small and the great, all peoples, races, tribes and tongues, all nations and all peoples everywhere on earth, who are and who will be, to persevere in the true faith and in penance for otherwise no one will be saved. [24]

What has preceded concerned the person as an individual. But every person and every Christian is part of a larger totality, a society and a community. Francis has a very keen awareness of the insertion of everyone in the community of the church, whether the earthly one with its ministerial structures or the heavenly one with its angels and saints assembled around the glorious Virgin Mary. Every time he addresses God—and there are some twenty prayers in his writings—one never hears only an individualistic prayer, but rather a plural and communitarian one.

Francis celebrates the mystery of the church on earth "our holy Catholic and Apostolic Church our mother" with its center in Rome, its hierarchy and its personnel. Like Mary, the Christian community, formed by people of every category, sex, race and in all times[25] is not only a social reality, but it is chosen by the Father, consecrated by the

Trinity and all the fullness of grace resides in it. Also, it is a *palace*, a *tabernacle*, a *dwelling* and a *garment of God* as well as its *mother* and *servant*. [26] Taking this dimension into consideration, Francis discerns and presents the different functions of the church. Its primary service is to be the space for faith and conversion: it is by it and through it that we receive the call to faith and undertake to change our lives. It is also the place for the presence of the Son of God for it is in it, through the ministry of priests, that the Body and Blood of Christ are rendered present. As criteria for true faith, it allows us to verify where we find ourselves in our personal faith. Since it also establishes norms of conduct, we must conform ourselves to even its disciplinary demands. "Holy Mother Church" with its heaviness and deficiencies is nonetheless more fundamentally the place for the presence of God, Christ, his gospel message and his sacraments, whence the deep and humble faith that Francis confers upon it.

The church on earth has its parallel in the glorious one in heaven. Beyond space and time, those who have preceded us already live a full and blessed life in the presence of God. The church in heaven, even if it escapes our experience, is in contact with our present experience: we are in communion with it, and we can reconnect with it by contemplation and intercession. It is made up of saints, our brothers and sisters—Francis knows and enumerates a certain number of them and the various categories—as well as the countless angels with Michael as their head.[27]

They form a marvelous crown for the Virgin Mary who is at its center. In Francis' spirituality, Mary holds an eminent place. Holy, glorious, virgin, mother, queen and servant, daughter of the Father, spouse of the Holy Spirit, Virgin made church, she is present every time Francis evokes the mystery of God and his activity in the world. She is something like a dividing line between the before and after, the gate through whom salvation entered the world. Francis dedicates two prayer-poems to her.[28] In them he admires Mary's grandeur, based on her election by the Father and her sanctification by the Son and the Spirit. She who lived as a servant gave to the Son of God "our human flesh and its fragility and who, with Him, chose poverty" remains a model for us to follow. Francis contemplates this model in its state of glory and sings of it while at the same time asking Mary to intercede for us.

Between these two churches there exists permanent circulation, even conviviality. The church on earth, sinful as it is, possesses a divine dimension which manifests itself fully in the communion of saints gravitating around the majestic icon of Mary, as Dante once penned, *umile e alta più che creature,* "the most humble and the most exalted of creatures." Men and women are inseparably part of both the heavenly and the earthly church.

Questions for Reflection

1. The way in which Francis presents the human condition is full of contrasts: images of God that are endowed with incomparable grandeur as well as poverty and moral misery. What Francis tells us of the human condition may shock us. How well does Francis' representation of the human condition correspond to human reality as you know it?

2. How do you think Francis would react to today's human condition?

3. What do you find most appealing or reassuring about the communion of saints and sinners?

NOTES

[1] *Francis of Assisi, Vol. 1, A Letter to the Entire Order*, v. 11, p. 117.

[2] *Ibid., Admonition 5,* v. 1, p. 131.

[3] *Ibid., Earlier Rule 23,* v. 8 p. 84.

[4] *Ibid., Earlier Rule 23,* v. 8 pp. 84–85.

[5] *Ibid., Second Letter to the Faithful,* v. 83, p. 51.

[6] *Ibid., Earlier Rule 17,* v. 6, p. 75; *Admonitions 2* p. 129; *12,* p. 133, *17,* p. 134.

[7] *Ibid., First Letter to the Faithful,* v. 36, p. 48.

[8] *Ibid., Earlier Rule 23,* v. 9, p. 85.

[9] *Ibid., A Letter to the Entire Order,* vv. 50–52, pp. 120-121.

[10] *Ibid., Prayer Inspired by Our Father,* v. 4, p. 158.

[11] *Ibid., Earlier Rule 17,* vv. 5–8, p. 75.

[12] *Ibid., Earlier Rule 23,* v. 1, p. 81.

[13] *Ibid., Earlier Rule 17,* v. 7, p. 75.

[14] *Ibid., Earlier Rule 22,* v. 6, p. 79.

[15] *Ibid., Earlier Rule 22,* v. 50, p. 81.

[16] *Ibid., Admonitions 5,* v. 3, p. 131.

[17] *Ibid., Earlier Rule 22,* vv. 9–17, pp. 79–80.

[18] *Ibid., Earlier Rule 11,* p. 72.

[19] *Ibid., Admonitions 27,* pp. 136–137.

[20] *Ibid., Admonitions 2,* p. 129.

[21] *Ibid., Admonitions 4,* p. 130.

[22] *Ibid., Admonitions 8,* p. 132.

[23] *Ibid., Earlier Rule 23,* v. 8, p. 84.

[24] *Ibid.,* v. 7, p. 84.

[25] *Ibid.*

[26] *Ibid., A Salutation of the Blessed Virgin Mary,* p. 163.

[27] *Ibid., Earlier Rule 23,* v. 6, p. 83.

[28] *Ibid., The Praises of God,* p. 109; *A Salutation of the Blessed Virgin Mary,* p. 163.

CHAPTER SIX

LIFE ACCORDING TO THE GOSPEL—AN ITINERARY

Almighty, eternal, just and merciful God,
give us miserable ones
the grace to do for You alone
what we know You want us to do
and always to desire what pleases You.
Inwardly cleansed,
interiorly enlightened
and inflamed by the fire of the Holy Spirit,
may we be able to follow
in the footprints of Your beloved Son,
our Lord Jesus Christ,
and, by Your grace alone,
may we make our way to You,
Most High,
Who live and rule
in perfect Trinity and simple Unity,
and are glorified
God almighty,
forever and ever.

Amen.

—*Letter to the Entire Order*[1]

In Chapter Two, we caught a glimpse of the abundant outpouring life of the Trinitarian God, what he is in himself and how he manifests himself in the world: Incarnation—Passion—Resurrection—outpouring of the Spirit. This God wants to give of himself by granting access to the richness of his being; and for this he creates, by his need to love, spiritual and bodily realities with the human person at the center and meant to be his partner. The latter is someone of grandeur, called to an unimaginable destiny, endowed with gifts and multiple energies. At the same time, human persons are incomplete, fragile and broken. Stricken with egoistic tendencies, tempted to affirm themselves as self-sufficient, they abandon themselves to these tendencies far too often and disfigure the image according to which they have been fashioned. A way of conversion, an itinerary is proposed to them: to turn their hearts toward God in love, adoration and praise; to practice a love of neighbor that is maternal; to live in the communion of the church and its sacraments; to experience and assume the radical poverty of their being; and to follow the footsteps of Christ that lead to the happiness of the Beatitude. Of such is their destiny and mission.

THE HEART TURNED TOWARD THE LORD

> Therefore, all my brothers, let us be very much on our guard that, under the guise of some reward or assistance, we do not lose or take our mind away from God. But, in the holy love which is God, I beg all my brothers, both the ministers and the others, after overcoming every impediment and putting aside every care and anxiety, to serve, love, honor and adore the Lord God with a clean heart and a pure mind in whatever way they are best able to do so, for that is what He wants above all else. Let us always make a home and a dwelling place there for Him who is the Lord God Almighty, Father, Son and Holy Spirit, Who says: *Be vigilant at all times and pray that you have the strength to escape the tribulations that are imminent and to stand before the Son of man. When you stand to pray say: Our Father in heaven.* And let us adore Him with a pure heart, *because it is necessary to pray always and not lose heart; for the Father seeks such* people who adore Him. *God is spirit and those who adore Him must adore Him in Spirit and truth.*[2]

"Let us love God, therefore, and adore Him with a pure heart and a pure mind, because that is what He seeks above all else…and day and night let us direct praises and prayers to Him, *for we should pray and not become weary.*"[3] When Francis traces a spiritual itinerary in his *Letter to the Faithful*, he indicates, as a priority, what is most essential: to love and adore God. This is the contemplative dimension of the Franciscan life, at once the root and the ultimate goal. If God abandons himself to us as his sons and daughters by a movement of holy love wherein he gives us everything he is and everything that burns in his heart, he "desires above all else" that we respond to him with our own love, our adoration, our praises and our service. To have "a pure heart turned toward the Lord" is a formula that is dear to Francis. It means that:

what is central, deepest, most unifying in our hearts must always remain awake to the desire and the search for God. This desire, this quest, must not remain on the level of empty words but rather must find expression through the multiple impulses and movements of our lives, through a love in which all our energies are involved: adoration, attitudes of awe, extreme reverence, interior prostration; praise wherein we marvel over God and his deeds, stammer when trying to express the inexpressible burning sensation of the encounter, and call upon all creation to jubilate. This is what is meant by *a pure heart*. At the origin of all prayer we find the Spirit of the Lord who dwells in the faithful and who, perfect adorer of the Father, produces in the heart of the believer an impetus toward God, a movement of "holy prayer and gift of self." [4]

Nothing better summarizes that which for Francis is the all-encompassing attitude that we are invited to have toward God than the following passage in which he addresses himself to all men and women and not only to a specialized category: "everywhere... and continually let all of us truly and humbly believe, and hold in our heart and love, honor, adore, serve, praise and bless, glorify and exalt, magnify and give thanks to the Most High and Supreme Eternal God Trinity and Unity, Father, Son and Holy Spirit." [5] A humble faith, a recollected heart (meditation), true love, deep respect, exuberant praise and thanksgiving—everything is said in this text, at once theology and poetry. This is what constitutes the Franciscan contemplative attitude.

"To cherish and nourish one's brother like a mother"

Francis never separates love of God from love of neighbor. This seems to him the primary requirement "of a life of penance," conversion and change. The will of God for us is "that we love him and we love our neighbor as ourselves."[6]

> Let each one confidently make known his need to another that the other might discover what is needed and minister to him. Let each one love and care for his brother as a mother loves and cares for her son in those matters in which God has given him the grace.[7]

> Let no brother do or say anything evil to another, on the contrary, *through the charity of the Spirit, let them serve and* obey *one another* voluntarily. This is the true and holy obedience of our Lord Jesus Christ.[8]

The neighbor is not only the brother who is near and with whom we are bonded because of our vocation and our life together. The neighbor is everyone with whom we come into contact: friend or foe, thief or bandit, all of whom one must receive kindly. It is the rich person whom one must not judge or scorn; the poor; the infirm; the sick; the lepers; the homeless whose company should make us rejoice; sinners to treat with mercy and without anger; and even those who treat us badly or think of us with ill will and whom we consider our enemies.

Love is not only a feeling, much less just a lot of words: "let us love, not in word or speech" (1 John 3:18). Meant to be real, love manifests itself primarily by conviviality and tenderness, with something maternal about it: attention to the other, a combination of affection and effective kindness. Toward all, considered as brothers and sisters, we will show ourselves as "meek, peaceful, modest, gentle, and humble, speaking courteously to everyone" without any will to power, like a brother or a sister, "a useless servant."[9] This basic kindness will incarnate itself in concrete, often material, gestures: responding to the daily needs of others, trying to put ourselves in their place; rejoicing in the good that others do as worthwhile as well as our own; and loving those who have become useless to us. [10]

To love others is never easy, especially when a sinner upsets us and contradicts our convictions, or our enemies threaten us and wound us. In the first case, regarding the evil that troubles us or makes us angry, we will oppose the sinner by a patient silence, not by making judgments or condemnations, very much aware of our own sins and weaknesses; we will above all put forgiveness and mercy into practice, something that Francis does address in a deeply moving *Letter to a Minister*. The love of enemies is the summit of the practice of neighborly love. In Francis' writings, he insists a great deal on this point. Jesus loved his enemies; he called the one who betrayed him a friend. To attain such a love—to love, bear with, forgive the one who annoys, tries, upsets and wounds us—is presented as the highest achievement of the presence and the action of the Spirit in us. [11]

LIFE IN THE CHURCH

> Afterwards, the Lord gave me, and gives me still, such faith in priests who live according to the rite of the holy Roman Church because of their orders that, were they to persecute me, I would still want to have recourse to them. And if I had as much *wisdom* as *Solomon* and found impoverished priests of this world, I would not preach in their parishes against their will. And I desire to respect, love and honor them and all others as my lords. And I do not want to consider any sin in them because I discern the Son of God in them and they are my lords. And I act in this way because, in this world, I see nothing corporally of the most high Son of God except His most holy Body and Blood which they receive and they alone administer to others.
>
> —*Testament*[12]

Until now we have treated the church as mystery. Now the concern is the attitude that we must have toward it, above all, toward those who are its official representatives and primary servants—the priests. Francis emphasizes the importance of the main sacraments of the church: the Eucharist and reconciliation.

Francis' writings speak a lot about priests. Their intellectual and moral life is not particularly exemplary in this era. Yet, the Christians must "venerate and revere the clerics, not so much for themselves, if they are sinners, but because of their functions."[13] We must love them and consider them as our "lords." It is not simply a question of tolerance, ecclesiastical diplomacy, but a faith requirement. "I do this," he writes, "because I see nothing other physically in this world of the Son of God, if not his Body and His Blood that the priests receive and administer… at the same time as they proclaim the Word of God, *spirit and life.*"[14] Ordained ministers make up the backbone of the body of the church by demarcating the space where the authentic Word of God can be heard and where the sacramental mystery of Christ is celebrated. To be in communion with them is indispensable, for they are the authentic safeguards of the goods of salvation.

Receiving the Eucharist was rare in Francis' time. Yet, he strongly recommended to all Christians, "put aside all care and preoccupation and receive the most holy Body and Blood of our Lord Jesus Christ with fervor in holy remembrance of Him"[15] In receiving, we remember, understand and revere the love that our Lord Jesus Christ had for us.[16] We must approach the Eucharist "with great humility and veneration," purely, orienting all our will toward God in order to please him and "holding back nothing for ourselves so that He Who gives Himself totally to us may receive us totally."[17] And we must do so without forgetting what is most important: the role of the Spirit in the reception of this sacrament (a notion that was an original contribution by Francis). "The Spirit of the Lord who dwells in the faithful is the one who receives the most holy Body and Blood of the Lord."[18]

The penance-confession of sins also has a place in Francis' vision. Knowing the human person to be fragile and sinful, he recommends its frequent practice, without forgetting that the sinner must be received with great mercy, that one must keep well hidden the sins of others, "*for those who are well do not need a physician, but the sick do.*"[19]

THE RADICAL POVERTY OF ONE'S BEING

Blessed are the poor in spirit, for theirs is the kingdom of heaven. There
are many who, while insisting on prayers and obligations, inflict
many abstinences and punishments upon their bodies. But they
are immediately offended and disturbed about a single word
which seems to be harmful to their bodies or about something
which might be taken away from them. These people are not poor
in spirit, for someone who is truly poor in spirit hates himself and
loves those who strike him on the cheek.

—Admonitions[20]

We find poverty constantly affirmed as the central point and the characteristic trait of Franciscan spirituality. The overall perspective that
we have just presented, in which a spirituality is a system formed of
multiple elements articulated according to a certain coherence,
excludes such a clear-cut affirmation. All the more so because the
poverty often attributed to the Franciscan path is seen mainly, if not
exclusively, from its material and social ramifications. However, even
if it were true that Francis made a radical choice of social poverty for
himself and his brothers, we would seriously misunderstand his
vision if we saw only this dimension of it that, moreover, he does not
propose to Christians living in the world. His conception of true
poverty that touches the very roots of one's being discloses unsus-
pected depths. Before manifesting itself in material poverty, which is a
kind of visible sacrament of it, poverty consists in three radical under-
takings: first, acknowledging that all goods belong to God; second,
admitting that only our evil and our afflictions belong to us; and
finally, carrying the cross of Christ each day, which means in being in

submission to everyone, in acceptance of rejection, sickness and death.

Who we are and what we can accomplish, above all when it consists of spiritual realities, is great and beautiful; it is legitimate to rejoice over it and be proud of it. But then a subtle temptation creeps in: *I am that which I speak of, it belongs to me. I am self-sufficient, I am like God.* In order not to fall into this temptation we must let go of this hold we have on the good that we do not own. Francis writes,

> I beg all my brothers…not to boast or delight in themselves or inwardly exalt themselves because of the good words and deeds or, for that matter, because of any good that God sometimes says or does or works in and through them.…

> Let us refer all good
> to the Lord, God Almighty and Most High,
> acknowledge that every good is His,
> and thank Him, "from Whom all good comes, for everything."[21]

To acknowledge the good that is in us is but a first step. Once this is done, one must strive to immediately refer it and return it to its true owner, God, the only good. The true and deepest poverty is to possess all things as a gift from God and not to have anything of one's own.

"We may know with certainty that nothing belongs to us except our vices and sins."[22] When we have acknowledged the countless gifts and goods that make up both who we are and what we have as God's property, and we have referred them to him in thanksgiving, what then is left for us to do? To be sure, God gives it all back to us as a pure and gratuitous gift, but then nothing belongs to us. Nothing other than, according to this very strong and hard saying of Francis, "our vices and our sins," or again, according to the quotation from Saint Paul, "our weaknesses."[23] We have seen, when we are treating that which is evil in the human person, how great are these weaknesses or infirmities and how we can become the plaything of our impulses and inclinations. Our poverty consists in the humble and merciful acceptance of this shadowy part of ourselves. To admit it, to suffer from it as a sickness, to seek to heal oneself of it, to cry out toward God our dire straits and await the heavenly doctor to deliver us, is the other face of poverty.

Francis' *Admonition 5*, so close in content to the beautiful text on perfect joy, indicates that after having cast aside all possible motivations for pride resting on human performance and on even the most elevated spiritual gifts, the only thing we "can boast in is our *weaknesses* and in carrying each day the holy cross of our Lord Jesus Christ" (v. 8). We know how weaknesses are to be understood, let us now see what our daily share in the cross of Christ requires: "we must rejoice, instead, when we fall *into various trials*, and, in this world, suffer every kind of anguish or distress of soul and body for the sake of eternal life."[24] What lies on the horizon for us, and which Francis evokes, is marked by suffering which no one can avoid and which the believers must assume for themselves in the following of the crucified Lord.

The suffering, the dysfunctional aspect of the human condition, is encountered every day in all kinds of circumstances. Thus, if one wants to be " a lesser one and subject to all"[25] one cannot avoid misunderstandings, opposition, even persecution. It can even happen that we will encounter rejections, very painful ones, from those closest to us, as did Francis himself as narrated in the story of True and Perfect Joy. And life itself is constantly threatened by sickness and, finally, death, two unavoidable companions, who sooner or later will come to visit us.

To Follow in the Footprints of Our Lord

> All my brothers, let us pay attention to what the Lord says: *Love your enemies* and *do good to those who hate you* for our Lord Jesus Christ, Whose footprints we must follow, called His betrayer a friend and willingly offered Himself to His executioners. Our friends, therefore, are all those who unjustly inflict upon us distress and anguish, shame and injury, sorrow and punishment, martyrdom and death. We must love them greatly for we shall possess eternal life because of what they bring us.
>
> —*Earlier Rule 22*[26]

To follow in the footprints of Jesus Christ is a theme that is very dear to Francis. It is even said that the following of Christ, the *sequela Christi*, characterizes Franciscan spirituality. This is true as long as we give an accurate content to this expression. This theme, borrowed from the First Letter of Peter,[27] does not speak of the deeds and gestures of the earthly life of Jesus that we would need to reproduce. It is rather an invitation to enter into, with tenderness and patience, the mystery of the blessed Passion of the Lord, and thus share in his painful and glorious destiny. Rather than a mystique of poverty understood in the sociological sense, the *sequela* is a mysticism of the Passion that in following the Lord finds its fulfillment in glory. To follow the footprints of Christ is to live according to all the demands of the gospel, suffering and death included, and to open ourselves to the promises that this gospel proclaims.

THE BEATITUDES AND THEIR FRUITS

Where there is charity and wisdom,
    there is neither fear nor ignorance

Where there is patience and humility,
    there is neither anger nor disturbance

Where there is poverty with joy,
    there is neither greed nor avarice

Where there is rest and meditation,
    there is neither anxiety nor restlessness.

Where there is fear of the Lord to guard an entrance,
    there the enemy cannot have a place to enter.

Where there is a heart full of mercy and discernment,
    there is neither excess nor hardness of heart.

—Admonition Twenty-Seven[28]

The path just described is a harsh and very demanding one. How can we follow it without feeling tense, without feeling sadness? Francis responds: "through patience, humility and joy which God himself possesses and which make up his being."[29] This joy can be experienced by meditating on the Word of God, which is a companion of poverty.[30] It can be so strong that it endures and keeps men and women in peace when they feel abandoned by everything. Francis invites his brothers to be "*joyful,* cheerful and consistently gracious *in the Lord.*"[31] Fifteen of the *Admonitions* begin with the exclamation: *blessed.* To be blessed in the midst of the difficulties and the trials of life is not possible without the presence of a mysterious inner reality: "humility and patience, the pure, simple and true peace of the spirit."[32]

Having reached this point, animated henceforth not by the spirit of the flesh, but by the "holy virtues which are poured into the hearts of the faithful through the grace and illumination of the Holy Spirit,"[33] men and women can look at the world around them with eyes purified like Francis who near the end of his life, in a particularly painful moment, composed his *Canticle of the Creatures*. This *Canticle*—a song of praise addressed to the almighty and good Lord whose name no human is worthy to mention and to whom alone glory and blessing belong—changes our way of looking at the order and the beauty of the fraternal world. From this perspective, everything is radiant with beauty and harmony: human wounds, trials, sickness, even death find their place—transfigured as they are by an invisible light. Initiated in painful struggle and hardship, the journey now opens up to share in the very life and joy of the Resurrection.

The Mission

> Listen, sons of the Lord and my brothers, *pay attention to my words. Incline the ear* of your heart and obey the voice of the Son of God. Observe His commands with your whole heart and fulfill His counsels with a perfect mind. *Give praise* to Him *because He is good; exalt* Him *by your deeds;* for this reason He has sent you into the whole world: that you may bear witness to His voice in word and deed and bring everyone to know that there is *no one who is all-powerful* except Him. Persevere *in discipline* and holy obedience and, with a good and firm purpose, fulfill what you have promised Him. The Lord God offers *Himself* to us as to His *children.*
>
> —*Letter to the Entire Order*[34]

When defining the mission of a human group in society or in the church, we try to describe what it does, its activity. Francis' texts, however, do not describe activities or services but the lifestyle of believers.

This is especially evident in the solemn text, filled with biblical associations, which opens the *Letter to the Entire Order* and constitutes the founding charter of the specific mission of the brotherhood. They are "sent into the whole world," commissioned "to bear witness to the Word" of the Son of God. The content of this message, inspired by Tobias's canticle used in the *Liturgy of the Hours*, is dense and lapidary: make known to everyone that "only God is all powerful." It is evocative of the great proclamation of the Koran, "God is great" that Francis must have heard from the minarets in Damietta, Egypt. But this all-powerfulness is not only or even primarily a creative force; it is kindness and love. "Proclaim that He is good and exalt him by your deeds." These deeds are not only outer achievements; they consist rather in a receptivity which may seem passive, linked to listening, as attested to by the four imperative phrases used: "listen," "pay attention," "incline your ear," "obey" and in the mention of the word "ear," by which is meant "the ear of the heart." It is the heart which receives the gospel message—the revelation of God, of his love, of his demands—and preserves the totality of this message: the commandments and the counsels, the fulfillment toward which one must persevere by "discipline, obedience, good and firm purpose." This message does not impose a heavy burden; it is not just a discourse, but also the encounter with someone who presents himself to us, as a father to his children.

According to the program laid out by this text, the mission of the brothers and sisters is proclaiming mainly through life example which words accompany and explain, the mystery of God—his all-powerful love and the discovery of what this accomplishes in the lives of men and women who open themselves to it: listening and receptivity to the Word, conformity to the Gospels, perseverance in fidelity. The heart of the mission—and the message—is here, and the rest of it, daily living and its structures, are at the service of this message.

THE LIFE OF THE WORLD TO COME

Your kingdom come:
That You may rule in us through Your grace
and enable us *to come* to *Your kingdom*
where there is clear vision of You,
perfect love of You,
blessed companionship with you,
eternal enjoyment of You.

—*Prayer Inspired by Our Father*[35]

Already in this life, the Christian who "perseveres in the true faith and in conversion," becomes the dwelling place and the temple of the Holy Spirit. The latter, finding his resting place in Christians, introduces them into the communion of the Father and the Son. Thus, having become themselves, sons of the Father, spouse, brother and sister of Jesus, they truly "become participants of the divine nature."[36] But this experience, which is the mystical summit of the Christian life, is lived out in the day-by-day obscurity of faith. Threatened by numerous obstacles,[37] it runs the risk of being forgotten and becoming commonplace.

Even today, Francis writes, the Father "dwells in the heavens, that is to say with the angels and the saints"; he is for them the light, love, beatitude. In cheerfulness,[38] they fully enjoy something of his being which is "sovereign, eternal good, from whom all good comes, without whom there is no good."[39] This full enjoyment is accessible only in the heavenly realm; for us, it is to come when in his glorious return, Christ will say to all those who have known the Father, adored Him and served Him in penance: "Come, you blessed of my Father, receive the kingdom prepared for you from the beginning of the world."[40]

God is "delightful and totally desirable above all else"[41] but Francis knows that this "delightfulness" is not continuous, but rather fluctuating and temporary. He prays so that purified, illumined and set ablaze by the fire of the Spirit, we can have access to it in this life and, following in the footprints of Christ, to finally attain the Father, the Most High, and share in his life, his kingdom and his glory.[41] Only then will God be seen as he is, loved as he is. Access to the Trinitarian communion will plunge us into the abysses of eternal happiness.[43]

Men and women will understand then what it means "to be saved by his mercy alone."[43] The Paradise of the delights of God, where he has placed them since the beginning and from which they have been in exile as the result of sin, will be reopened. After having endured in peace, sicknesses, anxiety, weariness, they can enter this Paradise to receive the crown of life. For Francis, the happiness of the world to come consists essentially in the vision and the love of the One who is "wisdom, humility, beauty, conviviality, joy and gladness"[46] and this in the joyful company of the throng of those who are saved.[47] Faced with such a destiny conceived and prepared by "the One who has loved us with a holy love, created us according to his image and likeness, has given us our body, soul, life, has redeemed us and will save us by his mercy alone,"[48] what can men and women do but sing:

Most High, all-powerful, good Lord,
    Yours are *the praises, the glory*, and *the honor*, and all *blessing.*
To You alone, Most High, do they belong
    And no human is worthy to mention Your name.

—*Canticle of the Creatures*[49]

Questions for Reflection

1. The gospel path that Francis proposes to us is very simple: turn our hearts toward God with love; adore and praise; love one's neighbor with a maternal love; live in the communion of the church; experience and assume the radical poverty of one's being; follow in the footsteps of Christ; and finally, discover the happiness of the Beatitudes. Such is our destiny and our misery. How do you now live out Franciscan spirituality concretely?

2. What do you still want or need to do to live out Franciscan spirituality more fully? What steps will you take to make this happen?

3. Who in your circle of family, friends, church members and neighbors do you think lives a Franciscan life? Why?

NOTES

[1] *Francis of Assisi, Vol. 1, A Letter to the Entire Order*, vv. 50–52, pp. 120–121.

[2] *Ibid., Earlier Rule 22*, vv. 25–36, p. 80.

[3] *Ibid., Second Letter to the Faithful*, v. 21, p. 47.

[4] *Ibid., Later Rule 5*, v. 2, p. 102.

[5] *Ibid., Earlier Rule 23*, v. 11, p. 85.

[6] *Ibid., Prayer Inspired by Our Father*, v. 5, p. 159.

[7] *Ibid., Earlier Rule 9*, vv. 10–11, p. 71.

[8] *Ibid., Earlier Rule 5*, vv. 13–15, pp. 67–68.

[9] *Ibid., Earlier Rule 3*, v. 11, p. 66.; *Later Rule 11*, v. 3, p. 106.

[10] *Ibid., Prayer Inspired by Our Father*, v. 5, pp. 158–159; *Admonitions 24*, p. 136.

[11] *Ibid., Later Rule 10*, v. 10, p. 105.

[12] *Ibid., Testament*, v. 6–10, p. 125.

[13] *Ibid., Second Letter to the Faithful*, v. 33, p. 47.

[14] *Ibid., Testament*, v. 10, p. 125.

[15] *Ibid., A Letter to Rulers of Peoples*, v. 8, p. 59.

[16] *Ibid., Prayer Inspired by Our Father*, v. 6, p. 159.

[17] *Ibid., A Letter to the Entire Order*, v. 29, p. 118.

[18] *Ibid., Admonitions 1*, v. 12, p. 129.

[19] *Ibid., Earlier Rule 5,* vv. 8, p. 67.

[20] *Ibid., Admonitions 14*, p. 133–134.

[21] *Ibid., Earlier Rule 23,* v. 7, p. 84.

[22] *Ibid., Earlier Rule 17,* vv. 6–7, p. 83–84.

[23] *Ibid., Admonitions 5,* v. 8, p. 132.

[24] *Ibid., Earlier Rule 17,* v. 8, p. 75.

[25] *Ibid., Earlier Rule 7,* v. 2, p. 68.

[26] *Ibid., Earlier Rule 22,* vv. 1–4, p. 79.

[27] 1 Peter 2:21.

[28] *Francis of Assisi, Vol. 1, Admonitions 27*, pp. 136–137.

[29] *Ibid., The Praises of God,* p. 109.

[30] *Ibid., Admonitions 27*, pp. 136–137.

[31] *Ibid., Admonitions 7, 16*, pp. 132, 134.

[32] *Ibid., Earlier Rule 17,* v. 15 p. 76.

[33] *Ibid., A Salutation of the Blessed Virgin Mary,* p. 163.

[34] *Ibid., A Letter to the Entire Order*, vv. 5–11, p. 116–117.

[35] *Ibid., Prayer Inspired by Our Father,* v. 4, p. 158.

[36] 2 Peter 1:4.

[37] *Francis of Assisi, Vol. 1, Earlier Rule 22,* vv. 9–26, pp. 79–80.

[38] *Ibid., Earlier Rule 23,* v. 26, p. 83.

[39] *Ibid., Prayer Inspired by Our Father,* v. 1, p. 158.

[40] *Ibid., Earlier Rule 23,* v. 4, p. 82.

[41] *Ibid., Earlier Rule 23,* v. 11, p. 85.

[42] *Ibid., A Letter to the Entire Order*, vv. 51–52, pp. 120–121.

[43] *Ibid., Prayer Inspired by Our Father,* v. 4, p. 158.

[44] *Ibid., Earlier Rule 23,* v. 8, p. 84.

[45] *Ibid., Canticle of the Creatures,* v. 10, 11, p. 114; *The Canticle of Exhortation*, v. 5, 6, p. 115.

[46] *Ibid., The Praises of God,* v. 4, p. 109.

[47] *Ibid., Earlier Rule 23,* v. 9, p. 84.

[48] *Ibid., Earlier Rule 23,* vv. 1, 2, 8, pp. 81–32, 84–85.

[45] *Ibid., Canticle of the Creatures,* vv. 1–2, p. 113.

BIBLIOGRAPHY

Brunette, Pierre, O.F.M. *Francis of Assisi and his Conversions.* Translated by Paul Lachance, O.F.M., and Kathryn Krug. Quincy, Ill.: Franciscan Press, 1997.

Chesterton, G. K. *St. Francis of Assisi.* New York: Image/Doubleday, 2001.

Cunningham, Lawrence. *Francis of Assisi: Performing the Gospel Life.* Grand Rapids/Cambridge: William B. Eerdman's Publishing Co., 2004.

Dalarun, Jacques. *The Misadventure of Francis of Assisi.* Translated by Edward Hagman, O.F.M. Cap. New York: The Franciscan Institute, 2002.

Francis of Assisi: Early Documents. Volume 1, The Saint. Edited by Regis J. Armstrong, J. A. Wayne Hellmann and William J. Short. New York: New City Press, 1999.

Frugoni, Chiara. *Francis of Assisi.* Translated by John Bowden. New York: Continuum, 1998.

Green, Julian. *God's Fool: The Life and Times of Francis of Assisi.* Translated by Peter Heinegg. San Francisco: Harper and Row, 1983.

Leclerc, Eloi, O.F.M. *Wisdom of the Poverello.* Translated by Marie-Louise Johnson, M.D. Chicago: Franciscan Herald Press, 1988.

Matura, Thaddée, O.F.M. *Francis of Assisi: The Message in his Writings.* Translated by Paul Barrett, O.F.M. Cap. New York: The Franciscan Institute, 1997.

Straub, Gerard Thomas. *The Sun and Moon Over Assisi.* Cincinnati: St. Anthony Messenger Press, 2000.

INDEX